D1383835

Ideas, Inventions, and Innovators

PEOPLE WHO CHANGED THE WORLD
POLITICS AND SOCIAL ACTIVISM

BY GRACE JONES

CRABTREE
PUBLISHING COMPANY
WWW.CRABTREEBOOKS.COM

CRABTREE
PUBLISHING COMPANY
WWW.CRABTREEBOOKS.COM

Published in Canada
Crabtree Publishing
616 Welland Avenue
St. Catharines, ON
L2M 5V6

Published in the United States
Crabtree Publishing
PMB 59051
350 Fifth Ave, 59th Floor
New York, NY 10118

Published in 2019 by Crabtree Publishing Company

Author: Grace Jones

Editorial director: Kathy Middleton

Editors: Kirsty Holmes, Petrice Custance

Proofreader: Melissa Boyce

Designers: Matt Rumbelow, Ken Wright

Prepress technician: Ken Wright

Print coordinator: Katherine Berti

Images

Shutterstock: Evan El-Amin cover (top left), title page (left), pp 5 (4th row, left), 24 (top); EQRoy pp 3, 17; Giannis Papanikos p 4 (top right); 1000 Words p 4 (2nd row, right); arindambanerjee p 4 (bottom left); neftali p 5 (2nd row, right); Alessia Pierdomenico pp 5 (3rd row, left), 18 (right); Jayakumar p 5 (3rd row, right); JStone pp 5 (4th row, middle), 26 (right); lev radin pp 5 (4th row, right) 28 (top); Philip Bird LRPS CPAGB p 9 (bottom); Nataliya Nazarova p 14 (left); Zvonimir Atletic p 14 (bottom); Everett Historical p 16 (left); p 18 (left); Radu Bercan p 18 (bottom); SAPhotog p 19 (bottom); Joseph Sohm p 20 (bottom); MoDOG p 21 (bottom); Matthew Conboy p 23 (left middle); Chris Parypa Photography p 24 (bottom); Heidi Besen p 25 (top); Evan El-Amin p 25 (bottom); Kathy Hutchins p 28 (bottom); Shawn Goldberg p 29 (top); Christopher Penler p 29 (middle);

Wikimedia: title page (top right), p 21 (top); title page (bottom right), pp 5 (top right), 10 (right); LOC pp 5 (2nd row, left); 12 (top right); Manfredo Ferrari pp 5 (2nd row, middle), 14 (top right); LOC pp 5 (3rd row, middle), 20 (right); p 6 (left); United States public domain p 7 (top); p 9 (top right); p 10 (left); p 12 (left); p 13; p 16 (top right); p 22; p 23 (bottom); p 26 (left); p 27; p 29 (bottom)

All other images from Shutterstock

All facts, statistics, web addresses and URLs in this book were verified as valid and accurate at time of writing. No responsibility for any changes to external websites or references can be accepted by either the author or publisher.

Printed in the U.S.A./122018/CG20181005

Library and Archives Canada Cataloguing in Publication

Jones, Grace, 1990-, author
        People who changed the world : politics and social activism / Grace Jones.

(Ideas, inventions, and innovators)
Includes index.
Issued in print and electronic formats.
ISBN 978-0-7787-5829-7 (hardcover).--
ISBN 978-0-7787-5972-0 (softcover).--
ISBN 978-1-4271-2240-7 (HTML)

        1. Political activists--Miscellanea--Juvenile literature.
2. Politicians--Miscellanea--Juvenile literature. 3. Social action--History--Miscellanea--Juvenile literature. 4. Political participation--History--Miscellanea--Juvenile literature. I. Title.

HN13.J66 2018   j361.2092'2   C2018-905466-2
                                                              C2018-905467-0

Library of Congress Cataloging-in-Publication Data

Names: Jones, Grace, 1990-
Title: People who changed the world : politics and social activism / Grace Jones.
Description: New York : Crabtree Publishing Company, 2019. | Series: Ideas, inventions, and innovators | Includes index.
Identifiers: LCCN 2018043636 (print) | LCCN 2018047139 (ebook) | ISBN 9781427122407 (Electronic) | ISBN 9780778758297 (hardcover) | ISBN 9780778759720 (pbk.)
Subjects: LCSH: Social justice--Biography. | Political activists--Biography.
Classification: LCC HM671 (ebook) | LCC HM671 .J66 2019 (print) | DDC 361.2092 [B] --dc23
LC record available at https://lccn.loc.gov/2018043636

CONTENTS

PEOPLE WHO CHANGED THE WORLD

· ·

Throughout history, human beings have made positive impacts on the world around them by having the courage to fight for change. Whether winning the right to vote for women or becoming the first black president of a country founded on slavery, people have accomplished great things in the name of justice and equality.

This book will profile just a few of the incredible people who have helped make the world a better place through their involvement in politics or social activism.

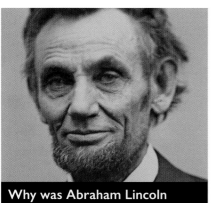

Why was Abraham Lincoln called "Honest Abe"?

How did Emmeline Pankhurst help get the vote for women?

Who was Mahatma Gandhi and what did he do for India?

How did Helen Keller overcome **adversity**?

How did Mother Teresa heal the world?

What did Rosa Parks do for **racial** equality?

What did Nelson Mandela do for South Africa?

How did Martin Luther King Jr. change civil rights?

Why did former Vice President Al Gore win the Nobel Prize?

Why was Barack Obama a very special president?

How is Malala Yousafzai helping girls attend school?

Who was the founder of the #MeToo movement?

Let's go on a journey to find the answers to these questions and more...

ABRAHAM LINCOLN

The 16th president of the United States is considered to be one of the most important leaders in history. With the **Emancipation Proclamation**, issued on January 1, 1863, and finally passed on December 6, 1865, Abraham Lincoln ended slavery in the United States. While African Americans would struggle for another 100 years to receive full rights in their country, Abraham Lincoln's actions marked an important **turning point** in the United States.

Wounded soldiers in Virgina in 1864, waiting to be treated after a battle during the Civil War.

Lincoln's popular nickname, "Honest Abe," shows how many Americans viewed him. Lincoln was widely considered to be trustworthy and to have high moral character. In his younger years, Lincoln was known to return money to customers who had overpaid him by mistake.

On November 19, 1863, Lincoln delivered a speech in Gettysburg, Pennsylvania, the site of one of the Civil War's major battles. Known as the Gettysburg Address, the speech is considered one of the greatest in history.

Abraham Lincoln won the presidential election in 1860. His antislavery views were well known, so very quickly after his election, the southern states that did not want to end slavery began separating from the country. Eleven states formed a new country, called the Confederate States of America. This led to the Civil War, which lasted from 1861 to 1865. To this day, the Civil War is the deadliest war Americans have witnessed. The war ended on April 9, 1865, when the Confederate States of America surrendered. Five days later, Lincoln was shot while attending a performance at a theater. He died on April 15, 1865.

"...that government of the people, by the people, for the people, shall not perish from the earth."
Abraham Lincoln, from the Gettysburg Address

EMMELINE PANKHURST

In the 1800s, women in many countries, including the United States, Canada, and Britain, began fighting for the right to vote. They felt women deserved a say in how their countries were run. In Britain in 1903, Emmeline Pankhurst formed a women's **union**. She and its members became known as suffragettes.

"Suffrage" means the right to vote in elections. Women's suffrage refers to the right for women to vote.

"We are here not because we are law-breakers; we are here in our efforts to become law-makers."
Emmeline Pankhurst

At first, the suffragettes used peaceful means of protest, such as marches. But after the British government continued to refuse them the right to vote, the protests became more passionate. Many women, including Emmeline Pankhurst, chained themselves to railings, broke store windows, and were arrested. The suffragettes were determined to win the right for women to vote. They hoped that the **publicity** caused by their arrests would help gain support for their cause.

People who were against women having the right to vote gave different reasons to support their argument, including the idea that women did not have the **intellectual** ability to make such important decisions, and that a married woman would vote as her husband did, so it would be like the husband getting two votes.

Pankhurst was very **influential** in the women's suffrage movements in the United States and Canada. She toured both countries and gave many lectures, encouraging women to fight for their right to vote.

Women marching in New York City in 1917. They are carrying banners with the signatures of one million women demanding the right to vote.

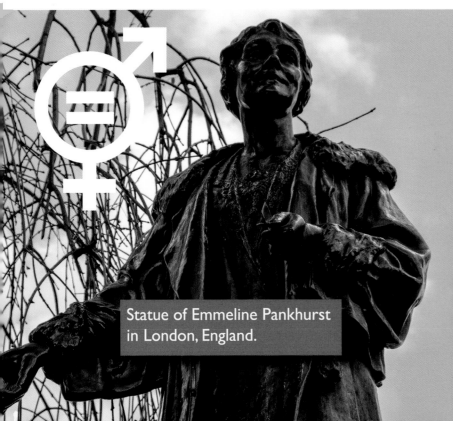

Statue of Emmeline Pankhurst in London, England.

Success finally came for Pankhurst and the suffragettes in 1918, when some women over the age of 30 won the right to vote. By 1928, all British women had the vote. Canadian women won the right to vote in 1918, while white American women received the right in 1920. Due to **racial discrimination**, black American women didn't win the vote until the passing of the Voting Rights Act in 1965.

MAHATMA GANDHI

Mohandas Karamchand Gandhi was born in 1948 in New Delhi, India, to a rich family. When he was 19 years old, he moved to England to study law at University College London. After his studies, Gandhi returned to India and opened a law practice, which was not successful. He took a job as a lawyer in South Africa, where he experienced racial discrimination.

At some point around 1915, people began calling Gandhi "Mahatma." This is an ancient Indian term which has a similar meaning to the English word saint.

Gandhi returned to India in 1915. His experiences in South Africa encouraged him to become a **civil rights** activist. At the time, India was part of the **British Empire**. This meant that Britain owned and controlled India and its people. Many Indians wanted independence from British rule.

Gandhi began to organize nonviolent protests against British rule. These were acts of **civil disobedience** which included things such as refusing to work. Gandhi was arrested and put in prison many times during this period. The British were afraid of how powerful he had become.

In 1930, when Britain raised the price of salt in India, Gandhi organized a march to the sea to make salt himself. Thousands joined him, marching 241 miles (388 km) from Ahmedabad to Dandi. Around 60,000 people were arrested, and the police beat many people.

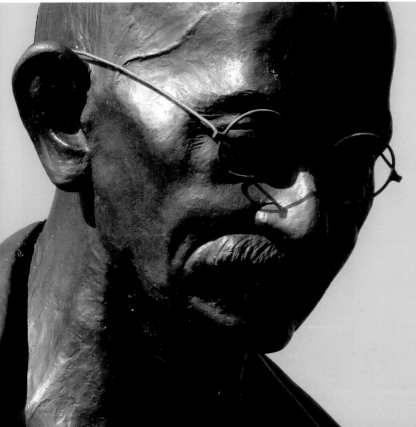

After many years of protesting and acts of civil disobedience, Britain eventually gave India independence in 1947. Sadly, Gandhi was shot and killed in 1948. He never saw India's official day of independence. To this day, Gandhi is admired as the leader of the Indian independence movement, who fought for freedom and equality through peaceful protest.

HELEN KELLER

Helen Adams Keller was born in 1880 in Alabama. At 19 months old, she became sick from an unknown illness, which left her blind and deaf. As she grew up, some people thought that Keller would never be able to learn, but her mother found a teacher named Anne Sullivan to help Helen.

Helen Adams Keller

Anne Sullivan

When Anne first met Helen, she brought her a doll. She put the doll into one hand and then pressed the letters of the word D-O-L-L into Helen's other hand. Even though Helen could learn the shape of the letters, she still did not know that the letters had any meaning to the object that she held in her other hand.

D-O-L-L

W-A-T-E-R

One day, Anne put Helen's hand under running water. Then she wrote the letters for the word water in Helen's other hand. Helen realized that meaning of the letters was connected to the running water she was feeling in her hand. That day, Helen learned many other words. Anne had finally taught her the connection between an object and its name.

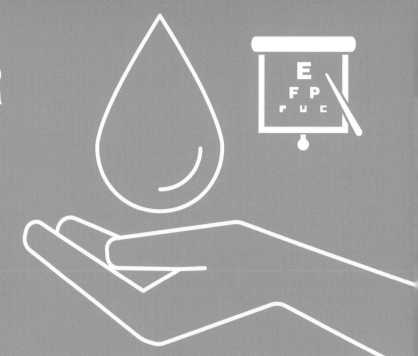

Helen Keller became the first college graduate who was deaf and blind.

Over 20 years, Anne taught Helen how to read entire books in **braille**, use a typewriter, and even to speak. Helen would touch a person's face to feel the sound vibrations and how their lips moved, and then copy them to make certain sounds.

As Helen grew older and learned more about the world around her, she wanted to help other people like her. She traveled around the country, giving speeches and raising money for charities that helped those who were deaf and blind. She also visited injured soldiers during **World War II** to spread a message of hope.

Helen Keller is an inspirational example of how determination, hard work, and belief can allow a person to triumph over adversity, no matter how many challenges they must overcome.

MOTHER TERESA

Mother Teresa was born in 1910 in Uskub, now known as Skopje, in modern-day Macedonia. She was raised as a **Roman Catholic**, and from an early age she wanted to become a nun and devote her life to helping others. When she was 18 years old she moved to India to become a **missionary** and a teacher.

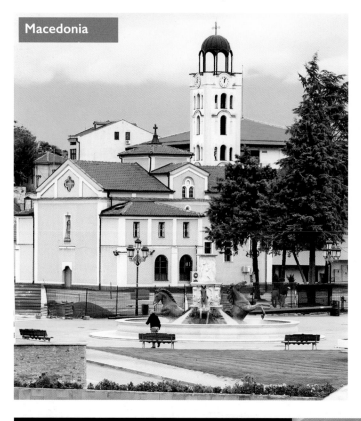
Macedonia

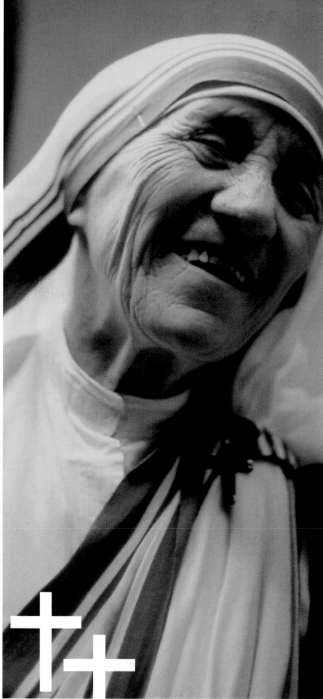

Mother Teresa saw many poor people suffering in India and felt inspired to help them. In 1950, Mother Teresa started a group called the Missionaries of Charity to help the sick and poor. She wasn't a rich woman and sometimes had to beg for food, but she still tried to feed and help some of the poorest people in India. She visited **slums** to provide food, and nursed those who were sick.

Under Mother Teresa, the charity grew, and nuns who were part of the organization traveled to other parts of India to help people in need. Other countries started to recognize Mother Teresa's work and began to follow her as an example of hope.

When the Missionaries of Charity first started there were only 13 members. Today, the group has over 4,000 nuns and 100,000 volunteers in 123 countries who continue to help people all over the world.

Mother Teresa set out to change the world and she did—through her faith, her message of hope, and her tireless work in caring for others. Mother Teresa and the Missionaries of Charity have saved thousands of lives around the world. After her death, she was declared a saint in 2016, and she is now known in the Roman Catholic Church as Saint Teresa of Calcutta.

1910– 1997

ROSA PARKS

Even though **slavery** had been **abolished** in 1865, in 1950s America, black people continued to suffer racial discrimination. **Segregation** laws meant that black Americans were not allowed to go to the same places that white Americans could, or they had to sit in different areas or rooms, separate from white people.

"Of course it felt like we should all be free people and we should have the same rights as other people." **Rosa Parks**

 Schools, restaurants, and restrooms are just some of the places where black people were segregated from white people.

In 1955, a 44-year-old woman named Rosa Parks refused to give her seat to a white passenger on the bus in which she was traveling in Montgomery, Alabama. She was arrested for breaking the segregation laws, and taken to jail. She was eventually released, but still had to pay a fine.

Rosa Parks' act inspired other black people in Montgomery to **boycott** the buses. This was an important moment in the beginning of the **civil rights movement**. The bus boycott was so successful that it continued for 381 days. When one of the protesters was taken to court, a judge ruled that segregated seating on buses was **unconstitutional**.

The Civil Rights Act of 1964 made segregation in schools, public places, and the workplace illegal.

At that time, 75% of people traveling on the buses in Montgomery were black.

 The Voting Rights Act in 1965 gave all black Americans the right to vote.

The Fair Housing Act of 1968 banned discrimination against people when they were looking to rent or buy houses.

'68

Rosa Parks is often called the "mother of the civil rights movement" because her bus boycott started a wave of protests across America.

The civil rights movement ended around 1968, by which time many laws had been passed to end segregation and achieve racial equality.

NELSON MANDELA

In South Africa in 1948, **apartheid laws** were passed. The apartheid laws meant that black people were discriminated against in all aspects of life. For example, black people could not live in the same areas, do the same jobs, or go to the same schools as white people.

Nelson Mandela was born in 1918 in Transkei, South Africa. When he was older, he thought apartheid was unfair so he became a civil rights activist in the anti-apartheid movement. He eventually joined the **African National Congress** party (ANC) and became very involved in the fight to end apartheid. In 1962, the South African government arrested him, and he spent the next 27 years in prison.

In prison, Mandela was treated very badly. He was forced to do backbreaking work every day. But he never gave up on his dream to end apartheid. In 1990, Mandela was released from prison, and apartheid laws slowly began to be abolished. In 1992, all people were given the right to vote. In 1994, the first **democratic** elections were held. The ANC won over 60 percent of the votes, and Nelson Mandela became the president of South Africa.

A new flag for South Africa was unveiled in 1994 (see right). The purpose of the new flag was to signal a new democracy in South Africa, and the end of apartheid.

Nelson Mandela fought against injustice and inequality throughout his life. He helped end apartheid and bring democracy and freedom to South Africa and its people. When Mandela died in 2013, leaders from around the world came to **commemorate** his life and achievements.

MARTIN LUTHER KING JR.

Born in 1929 in racially segregated Atlanta, Georgia, Martin Luther King Jr. learned early on that black people were treated differently in America. When he was six years old, his best friend was white. When they started school, they had to attend different schools, because of segregation. Then his friend's father stopped them from playing together.

King grew up feeling a strong need to help others and create positive change. He became a **Baptist** minister and planned to serve his community that way, but very soon, King became the most important leader in the civil rights movement.

Every year, on the third Monday of January, Martin Luther King Jr. Day is celebrated as a national holiday.

In 1955, when Rosa Parks refused to give up her seat on the bus in Montgomery, Alabama, King became one of the leaders of the bus boycott. Many white people were angry at the idea of ending segregation. King's house was bombed as a warning for him to stop the boycott. Instead, King became the national face of the civil rights movement.

After the Montgomery bus boycott, King became one of the main leaders of the civil rights movement. He fought for racial equality using peaceful protest rather than violence. In 1963, Martin Luther King Jr. helped to organize a huge **March on Washington**, which was attended by more than 250,000 people. It was there that King gave his famous speech, "I Have a Dream."

In 1964, the Civil Rights Act passed. That same year, Martin Luther King Jr. was awarded the **Nobel Peace Prize**. In 1968, he was shot and killed. More than 100,000 people lined the streets to pay their respects during his **funeral procession**. Today, King is remembered for his dedication to the civil rights movement and his work to end racial discrimination.

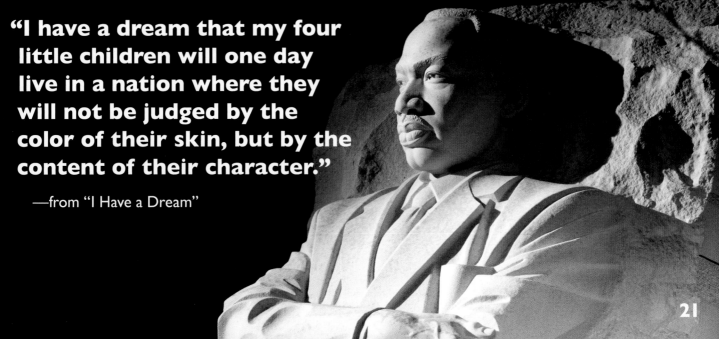

"**I have a dream that my four little children will one day live in a nation where they will not be judged by the color of their skin, but by the content of their character.**"

—from "I Have a Dream"

AL GORE

Climate change is widely discussed now, but when Al Gore began talking about climate change as a United States congressman in the 1970s, it was not. Throughout the 1980s, when he was a senator, and the 1990s, when he was vice president of the United States, Al Gore worked to raise awareness about the dangers of **global warming** and **climate change**. However, Gore's greatest contribution to environmental activism occurred after he left politics.

Global warming

before   now   after

In 2006, the documentary film *An Inconvenient Truth* was released. The film follows Al Gore as he travels around presenting a slideshow he created to educate citizens about the dangers of global warming and climate change. The film was an international box office success. It won two Academy Awards, and is credited with significantly raising international public awareness about environmental concerns.

IT may BE INCONVENIENT BUT it's the TRUTH NO ALTERNATIVE FACTS ABOUT CLIMATE CHANGE!

In a 2007 survey of citizens from 47 countries who had seen *An Inconvenient Truth*, 66 percent said the film had changed their mind about global warming, 89 percent said the film had made them more aware of the problem, and 74 percent said they had changed some of their daily habits after seeing the film.

Today, Gore continues his environmental work. He runs The Climate Reality Project, a **nonprofit** organization dedicated to climate change awareness and activism that is operating in more than 30 countries. In 2017, the film *An Inconvenient Sequel: Truth to Power* was released.

In 2007, Al Gore received the Nobel Peace Prize in recognition of his work to draw worldwide attention to the dangers of global warming and climate change.

BARACK OBAMA

• •

Barack Obama was born in Hawaii in 1961 to a black father and a white mother. Obama was intelligent and worked hard at school. After finishing college, he moved to Chicago to do community work, such as job training and advising on tenants' rights . He eventually gained a place in law school at Harvard University.

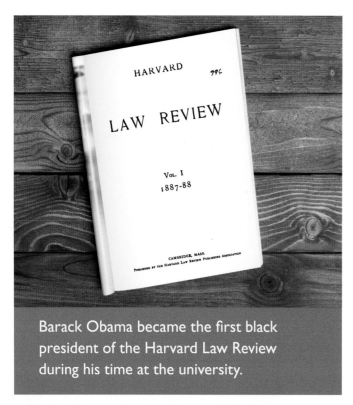

Barack Obama became the first black president of the Harvard Law Review during his time at the university.

After graduating from law school, Obama taught law in Chicago. He also joined the Democratic Party. In 2004, he was elected to the United States Senate. In 2008, he decided to enter the race for president of the United States. On January 20, 2009, Barack Obama officially became the first black president of the United States. In a country founded on slavery, this was a hugely important victory.

The Democratic Party believes in equality, human rights, freedom, peace, and justice.

During Obama's eight years as president, his many achievements resulted in changes in American society, the **economy**, and America's relationship with the rest of the world. He passed a set of laws that gave medical insurance to many people who could not previously afford it. He also is considered to have turned a failing economy into a successful one.

Obama started the process of withdrawing all soldiers from Afghanistan and Iraq where they had been fighting wars for a number of years.

Obama is remembered as being a likable, **dignified**, and hardworking president. In 2009, he was awarded the Nobel Peace Prize for his effort to strengthen cooperation between people.

MALALA YOUSAFZAI

Malala Yousafzai was born in the Swat Valley region of Pakistan in 1997. As she grew up, she noticed that many girls around her did not go to school. Her own father ran a school for girls and encouraged her to follow her ambitions to become a teacher, doctor, or politician.

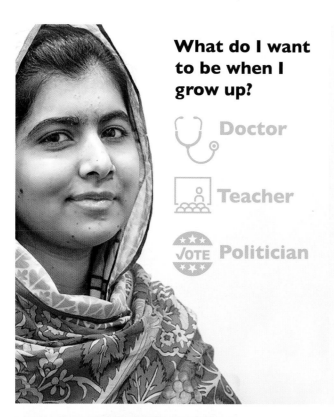

"When the whole world is silent, even one voice becomes powerful."
Malala Yousafzai

What do I want to be when I grow up?

Doctor

Teacher

VOTE Politician

When Malala was around ten years old, a group called the **Taliban** began to take control of the region where she lived. The Taliban said that women should stay at home, and schools for girls were shut down. Malala began to speak out on a blog about the bad things the Taliban was doing. The blog was very popular, and even though Malala wrote under a fake name, the Taliban discovered she was the writer and began sending death threats to her and her family.

BLOG

One day in 2012, Malala was returning home from school on a bus. The bus was stopped and a member of the Taliban identified Malala and shot her. The bullet went through her head, neck, and shoulder. Malala was seriously injured, and was flown to a hospital in England. However, she recovered and was back at school in England within six months.

As soon as she had recovered, Malala immediately continued to talk and write about equal rights and education rights. Her refusal to be silenced has brought hope to millions of people around the world who do not have access to education and are **oppressed** by others.

Malala Yousafzai was the youngest person to receive the Nobel Peace Prize in 2014.

TARANA BURKE

In 2006, American civil rights activist Tarana Burke began a nonprofit organization called Just Be Inc. Her goal was to help young women of color deal with the trauma of sexual abuse. Burke looked for a motto that symbolized the **empathy** and **empowerment** she hoped to share with the girls. She decided to use the phrase "me too."

 In a survey conducted in January 2018, 81 percent of women and 43 percent of men said they had experienced sexual harassment or assault in their lifetime.

On October 5, 2017, news broke of multiple **allegations** of **sexual harassment** and assault against the powerful Hollywood producer Harvey Weinstein. On October 15, the actress Alyssa Milano invited people who had experienced sexual harassment or assault to use the phrase "me too" on social media. That same day, the **hashtag** #MeToo went **viral**, proving that sexual harassment and assault is a major problem around the world. It was soon discovered that Tarana Burke had actually begun using the phrase more than ten years earlier. Burke is now credited as the founder of the powerful #MeToo movement.

The #MeToo movement has grown quickly, as more and more sexual assault survivors around the world come forward to share their stories. One of the most important ways the #MeToo movement is causing change is in how survivors are being treated. Sexual assault and harassment survivors are often shamed, ignored, or not believed. But due to pressure and awareness caused by the #MeToo movement, this is beginning to change.

On September 27, 2018, Dr. Christine Blasey Ford testified before the U.S. Senate about the sexual assault she says Supreme Court nominee Brett Kavanaugh committed against her. This was an important moment in the #MeToo movement, not only for Blasey Ford's courage in coming forward, but for the respectful way she was treated during the testimony process. Tarana Burke described Blasey Ford's testimony as a **tipping point**, and is hopeful the #MeToo movement will continue to inspire positive change.

"It's not about a viral campaign for me. It's about a movement. On one side, it's a bold declarative statement that 'I'm not ashamed' and 'I'm not alone.' On the other side, it's a statement from survivor to survivor that says 'I see you, I hear you, I understand you, and I'm here for you or I get it.'"
—Tarana Burke

GLOSSARY

abolished Put an end to something

adversity A difficult situation

African National Congress After apartheid, South Africa's ruling political party

allegation A claim that someone has done something wrong

apartheid laws In South Africa, government-enforced rules of racial discrimination and segregation

Baptist A branch of Christianity

boycott To stop using goods or services as a means of protest

braille A system of writing and printing using a combination of dots and points which allows people who are blind to read by touch

British Empire World territories controlled by Britain, from 1500s to 1900s

civil disobedience The refusal to comply with certain laws as a peaceful form of protest

civil rights The rights of citizens to political and social freedom and equality

civil rights movement Organized activities in the 1950s and 1960s that demanded racial equality for black Americans

climate change A change in weather patterns around the world

commemorate To remember and show respect for someone or something

democratic Relating to freedom, equality, and government by the people

dignified Calm and serious, worthy of respect

economy The wealth and resources of a country

Emancipation Proclamation A law issued on January 1, 1863, freeing all enslaved people in the United States

empathy To share and understand the feelings of someone else

empowerment To become stronger and more confident

funeral procession The route traveled taking a deceased person to their place of rest

global warming The gradual increase in the temperature of Earth's atmosphere

hashtag A word or phrase that begins with the symbol #, classifying it for social media

influential Having the power to cause change

intellectual The ability for intelligent thought

March on Washington The political demonstration held on August 28, 1963 in Washington, D.C. demanding civil rights for black Americans

missionary A person sent by the church to carry out charitable work

Nobel Peace Prize An annual prize for outstanding work in the name of peace

nonprofit An organization that does not seek to make a profit

oppressed Cruel or unjust restrictions put upon a person by an authority

LEARNING MORE

publicity Attention given to something by the media

racial Relating to race, or individuals with a common ancestor

racial discrimination To treat people unjustly due to their race

Roman Catholic A branch of Christianity

segregation The act of separating people into groups, sometimes based on race

sexual harassment Unwanted touching or remarks of a sexual nature

slavery The practice of being a slave or owning slaves

slums Heavily populated and run-down parts of cities in which poor people live

Taliban An Islamic extremist political and military organization

tipping point When a series of incidents becomes significant enough to cause important change

turning point The moment when a course of events is changed significantly

unconstitutional Something that goes against the principles which govern a country

union An organization of people working together to protect or further their rights

viral On social media, when a post or hashtag becomes widely shared

World War II A global conflict that lasted from 1939 to 1945

BOOKS

Kopp, Megan. *The Civil War*. Crabtree Publishing, 2018.

Ridley, Sarah. *Suffragettes and the Fight for the Vote*. Franklin Watts, 2017.

Spence, Kelly. *Malala Yousafzai: Defender of Education for Girls*. Crabtree Publishing, 2017.

Staton, Hilarie. *Civil Rights*. Crabtree Publishing, 2015.

WEBSITES

Visit this site to learn about the amazing people who have been awarded the Nobel Peace Prize:
https://kids.kiddle.co/Nobel_Peace_Prize

Learn more about the Civil War here:
https://www.battlefields.org/websites-kids

This website is full of interesting facts and information about climate change:
https://climatekids.nasa.gov/climate-change-meaning/

INDEX